THE MIDDLE WEST

Poems by

Danny Rendleman

arts foundation of michigan

Together... Investing in the Creative Spirit

Published by The Ridgeway Press
P.O. Box 120
Roseville, MI 48066

Publisher: M. L. Liebler

For Janice,
with celebration and desire.

*

Grateful acknowledgement to the following publications where these poems were first chosen to appear, often in different form:

Abraxas: "Muskegon."
American Poetry Review: "Looking Back on the Avant-Garde."
Artifact: "Narcissus."
Brix: "The Painter Apologizes to His Muse."
Chiaroscuro: "Tricks of the Stylish."
Cutbank: "Family, Easter Portrait, 1952."
5 A.M.: "Press."
Kwasind: "1945," "Write Me a Poem About China."
The Literary Magazine: "Cold Motions."
The MacGuffin: "The Cardinals."
o-blek: "Poem Beginning With a Line by Janice."
Passages North: "Cheese Lines" and "Scripture."
Poetry Now: "The Draggers."
Raccoon: "Rosalie."

"Looking Back on the Avant-Garde" was reprinted in *Industrial Strength Poetry,* copyright 1984 by Art Army Press, Inc.

"Charlie" and "Tremor" are from *Contemporary Michigan Poetry: Poems From the Third Coast,* copyright 1988 by Wayne State University Press, Inc.

"Daguerre" appeared as a broadside from OtherWind Press, copyright 1987.

My appreciation to the Faculty Development and Awards Committee at the University of Michigan-Flint and to the Office of the Vice President for Research at the University of Michigan, Ann Arbor for the support of this publication. Additional thanks to the Michigan Council for the Arts and the Arts Foundation of Michigan.

CONTENTS

THE MIDDLE WEST

LOCUS CERULEUS

JANICE AT THE PIANO

1.

It is late enough in winter's evening
I can't see out the windows, see only
my reflection and a far-off tungsten light
through the snow-loaded trees, hear
the wind lowly moaning, the furnace clicking
and chugging away below us, and a few bars
of faulty Brahms, a singular line of chords
fingering out, tentative as an ember,
smoke from a coal, a twig at the glass
already imagining the machinery of fire to come.

2.

Next to last ruckus of winter this March morning:
my room surrounded by the iced patina
of nothing doing, the blowsy sky a parquet
of blue and blah--as mixed a metaphor as the month is
    long.
Today it is the hymns of Fanny J. Crosby,
blue-black with the bruise of God.
The world waits, secure in its summer promise,
gold and hot as bourbon in a cold blue goblet.

3.

I wake sweating from dreams in the yellow morning,
I turn down the radio to hear your piano sing.
My father used to say
a lot of worthless things, but he used to say
the world will do its best to nickel and dime you
to death. Within this music you heave
into the void is that dead language, one more facet
of that longing, putupon room of our being,
love, our terror of love and its crime of passion.

SWAY

"To describe how many various shapes
   affrightened imagination represente things to me in."
                                              --Daniel Defoe

1.
To suppose in your absence something
would make itself known to me: gull cry,
imprint of a voice of humid air
like a signet in blue wax. Not exactly
addled to assume--while the small agony
of your last words shimmered around me,
etching in me--that every new sad minute
coming along

(laps of foam inching up the littered beach)

would offer respite, never before seen,
conceived, flow of dissipation in driftwood,
or emptied orange crabshell, this mollusk, that.

All these relics curled around air
like your ear without my song,
your toes without my tongue; knee, navel,
vagina, eyelid around the chimera.

You see, far as the eye can capture,
all these shibboleths, by-words,
down the sand as far as Vancouver,
haints, ghosts, memory. Return and you'll find
only a cup of desire, a cup of fiction.

I'll give these forms a reason to be,
if you'll be so kind. Out the window,
children's voices, their bodies floating away.
If, so.

2.

And if so, what recollection will I allow
to jell, will have bronzed and tottering
on my dashboard, driving all night into the rest
of my otherwise sensible life? I ask you.

Just this, just so:
You so very angry with the terrorizing earth,
it so hot sleep had become a birth-mangled
cat whose head you smashed but would not die--

that convoluted, that over-wrought
an image that fits, as we fit each other.
You, so pissed at a world of tedium and spite
and dreary rage, you glowed and spun
in the sheets as no wind blew, a trickle of sweat
between your breasts. Sweet river, I wanted to say
and you knew it--why else the book
aimed at my head?

3.
To hold sway: It's no crime. We keep trying
until we get it right, like sunsets, good graces,
sympathy. Take one hundred million bland gestures
we dish out every day, the mild blond furniture
of our by-your-leaves, or say-so. Naught.

Oh, la.
Oh, life almost goes on--petty, manic, shot
through with the sear of despair though it may be.

But, then you articulate that spine of yours,
that skull, antic as those dream parts of us
animals recognize when they look long at us
and shiver and sleep again.

HOW BIRDS MOVE

1.
The Robin

Big as a squab, he comes
to drink at my rain gutter.
Cocks his head at the cat,
the late afternoon sun, me.
Fat with not insects or seed
but worms, he waddles,
thinks darkly and takes our time.
Near the feeder for the others,
two butterflies samba and slide,
bothering a squirrel content
to graze among the leavings,
a squirrel my wife insists
on calling Maurice. That is,
I suppose it's him. The robin
lifts off into his greenery
at the sharp retort of door slam.
Evening, all my friends, is nigh.
How is it, my friends, we hope
to discover what to perhaps
do next among the familiar,
the old slants of sun on ready surfaces?
The oak leaf flat as a face,
the jerry-rigged planters
of railroad ties hatcheting the light,
the orbs and wedges of bird song?
Dog bark, dog bark, dog?
Even this cool May air,
holding aloft gnats and various
seedlings is like hands on the brow,
fingers on pulse, a beckoning.

2.
The Grackel

Slick as oil, as emeralds,
he slides through the long grass,
alone as a soul
this evening bell tolls for.
Spastic, colon-colored, bird of filth--
cousin of the crow--yet taking up
just the right amount of air,
his yellow eyes in a sea of grime,
neither of them ever seeing
the same thing. He not so much
struts as parlays his darkness
into the old bait and switch.
Good bird. You're after my heart.

3.
The Finch

There, then not there.
But yellow, yellow, yellow
and black. The small
swoop, the density of small needs,
the severe but tangent song
of one doomed to a short life
and small. Finch: like a bright
cipher at the feeder,
eating its weight in thistle seed
daily, a blip, a no-account
glitch in the garden.
Save us all, bird. Be the spark
that is the next moment,
would we have it.

4.
The Mourning Dove

In my wishfulness,
I trust they are grim mates for life,
and imagine them amiably stupid.

They bob their precise, oiled way
around our amateur compost pile,
ponderous, blithe, in love.

But we are struck by
such mild, saintly birds folding
their evening robes so lordly,

slowly, around them, around and about
even us.
Why do they move as they do?

Some say it's physical, others
that it's but gravitational pull.
Their small heads,

their smaller, lamentable hearts--love,
lack of intelligence, earth's suck:
Thankfully, it's all the same.

CITY POEM

Ease of our several familiar skins on skins,
of how we self-slick, to make it all that much
more predictable, satisfying, or not,
but at least endearing, sizzling in the memory,
win or lose. Language melds us, two into one,
language of sex, vice-versa, so to speak,
fusion, suckings and groanings as of
a lightless fen sending forth intimations
of sensate beings: not yet. Wouldn't it just be . . . ?
Soup and sympathy, regards to all, the rest.
All the rest. Only the remembered dread
of a father: up in the middle of the night to piss,
wavering in the lit doorway, looking at you
as though you were edible, dying in a week.

All this talk of what you might be missing--
children, fame, money enough to dawdle in sea-foam,
in the middle of your novel. You look away,
shake your head as if to say, Oh, Christ,
stuck with an asshole once again in Bijou-land.
Suddenly everything is happening--lawn mowers, sirens,
the hot fat of the pork is flaring into flame.
I swear, in the last ten minutes I've seen three
transport planes. Maybe it was the same one.
But still . . . . You look up from the chops on the grill
to me: Did you read that there's a suicide
every twenty minutes? I say, Do you know
what butterfly pork chops are made of? Since June
first we have heard the same unearthly moaning.

This is a day we'll remember for its pastels:
the gray cat twining through wrought-iron, the basil
and true lavender in their pots. A day promising
rain like a frazzled father promising his boy
a game of catch. After dinner. First thing. Soon.
It smells like the first day of summer, you say.
It is the first day of summer. At one time, she says,
I thought it important to know what those other
instruments beside the sitar were called. Clouds
dissipate. Don't we all? Look:

I'm not about to go defining my love for you.
I'm just going to verb my way along, hope for the best,
sleeping, raging, prying my body
open for whatever suggestions come to mind.
Fuck your finches and your cats with names
I'm embarrassed to call out into the evening clothes
of evening. Let me lie with you, stretching
our forgotten organs of flesh taut against one another,
the plum and swooning air upon the hills around this
city we're one with, willing victims that we are.

MUSKEGON

In your eyes is that patch of ice
I want my wheels to hit,
while the first taut buds of the year
hum their muzzy tunes. Every part of you
fits my hands the way, at one time,
prayer fit ambition. I want to tell you
about a river that is no symbol,
a river that stands for nothing.
I was sitting on its edge,
on the rim of November, the leaves
so thick in it, I could have walked across.
Down the road my mother was folding
old letters into her white Bible,
tucking in the last hoopla of her life,
and my father watched for white-tails
out the trailer window in up-north Michigan.
I listened to the long vowels of cedar
and jackpine invent winter all over again.
But I was smiling, trying to make sense
of it all, of some of it, one word of it.
And I wanted you, a woman like you
to sing by the fire, as now,
about automobiles and the women
that gasoline and music could buy.
I didn't know who you were yet, being
merely prescient and lonely, as were we all.
Now, we wade into life with exclamation
and cheap joy, while the moon, that old newsboy,
looks down upon us with his nearly genuine,
nearly sympathetic eye.

LOOKING BACK ON THE AVANT-GARDE

So, the movies called you away, as the memory
of certain simple dresses still do, pleasant
flowered devices flung on the end of your bed,
or, there, reflected in the mirror, hanging
by the open window, enjoying the Great
Outdoors in its private way. Or is it that
we want to get through more space, through
less time? More love or fewer pristine miseries--
scabbed knees, forgotten favors, a delicacy
we can no longer comfortably afford. You find it
less and less difficult to get from the individual
noises of dawn to those of dusk, the harmony
you have no control over, and so the most pure.

The most revealing calamity you discovered that day,
of course, was that there could also be green apples
with salt, the accidental epiphany of skin
on skin, hand-me-down sweaters with small figures,
strange linen, strange views of the moon. But
these were givens, like the taste of your breath
rollicking out and up to all those sheriff badges
in the nearly familiar sky. Life come down to this:
We imagine each tree as flow, as running sustenance.
Like every boy in every song lighting up your eye.
Like leaving home, going around shutting off
electricity so it won't be unhappy without you.
Azaleas shatter and strew your path with white jewels,
marvelous gestures in your plucky, American adventure.

COLD MOTIONS

Is this to be just another chill night
of querulous dogs, the moon a yellow globe
trailing down the rutted road,

beneath these always cumulous clouds, this
tremulous sky, the insects finally as still
and dumb as money under rocks?

We walk back from the garden
through soaked leaves like dark bandages,
the summer greenery becoming firewood.

Perhaps our only knowledge is of how
forms may be fit into, slung together flush,
and a certain grand sorrow for it all.

Today, the sunless last light climbs
the patterned stairs on our heels
as we smell the drugstore soap of each other.

Nothing is secure. Where is the taste of us
is all this, these baskets of wind aloft
on the avenue, cool diaries of late blooms?

The radio says the trees have peaked
in their hysteria, there is nothing more to see.
We, too, urge what we cannot use out of us.

Then we use it.

THE CARDINALS

What is this melody to which we shape
our dance, the bass and rhythmic intricacy?
you say, "Come see the cardinals at the feeder,
so unmistakable, they must know we watch."
Who are these claret birds of omen in the snow,
these jots of wine on china?

We draw the shades against sight,
against the whirl of new snow . . . we move
in our love like drifts of warmth, gold on water,
mystery mingling with the pedestrian.

We are led to believe it will storm.
We make do with what we get--enough wind
to shake the candle flame. Are we not
powerless but to do the best we can?
Thus, our hands bent around the brittle
yet fluent fire, the clay and spit
of our bodies pried loose
to caulk the other vast but careless lives
outside our daily concern.

Like a blue tattoo above us,
the Archer wheels across this temperate sky,
his eye the eye of killer and prey,
bright with intention and fear, his skin
the form of dream leaving dreamer behind,
impatient with sleep's addiction.

We live, we guess, with one thing in mind:
to survive alone, if need be, in the middle
of the night, the glowing points of our bodies
flaring apart, peopling the dark soup of waning stars.

14

We ease from sleep, the way it is possible
to say the word <u>grace</u> and mean nothing more
than the smell of ourselves at our human best,
loving, waking like old leaves just now splayed
in the brave winter sun, leathery and odd.

The cats in the window stare and murmur
with us, their round, savage eyes dilated with hunger,
amazed at such sudden reeling flight
of birds the color of our hearts.

MATH IN PROVIDENCE

Out the window Rhode Island begs to be
remembered to you within a similar
place--dark brick, jumbled sky,
and high wind up to no good.
I want to tell you how it's been,
to translate the weather and the bruise
of your absence into a magic
that will transform you, too, make
you want to be here now, serene as amber.

But reality persists, as always.
The bare trees remain so, throwing out
their angled arms to the mist,
as the daily grind ticks past, beyond
possession or memorial, the way
celebration of the commonplace sours
to a film. Here, city fathers
gut the train station for commerce.
I can see the diamond torches flitting
like canaries in a cave, the morning traffic
pearling along I-94, headlights at five a.m.
of people going to work, coming home
from third-shift jobs in truck plants,
coffee on their shortness of breath.

In the hotel rooms around me,
someone listens to the early news that makes us
whimper for one bit of grace.
Someone shaves, someone yells at someone crying,
"Oh, please, no, please." A door slams. . .
You might like to know, I got my hair cut
in the barber shop here in the lobby
that smelled of pomade, lilac, and dry heat.
I sat biding my time amid magazines curling,
portly men talking loudly about their ladies
and their cunts. The snow of Providence
clicked on the plate glass etched with curlicues
advertising SHINE!

I was ready to believe any stranger with a tale,
to hear I was in a childhood place, vibrating
like an edge in someone's memory, even my own.
I half-expected my father to come out from
the back room, having shared a joke and a Schnapps
with the owner. It was not to be, you might
like to know, though I held myself very still.

Let us solve for X.

Let X equal us. Let us plot the unknown accurately,
in the middle of our souls, the hand striking flesh,
the spit oath, the rage against calm
marrowing even the smallest bones of our bodies.
I want you and the life we were whittling together,
shaping the intangible breath between us.
I want our vagaries to interlock like fingerprints,
rivers of precision, sculpting the air
that lovers make disappear between them,
solving for zero.

WRITE ME A POEM ABOUT CHINA

she said.
Write me what you hadn't thought of
until you met me,
round as an egg and blue.

Put in some decent big skies, too,
some dazzle. No more thighs,
please, no more thigh bones
or dead relatives,
lounging about like musty wine bottles
or yellowing news-clippings.

No more melt or damp
or wet or sop or sog.
Make it glitter, sun on mica,
the yellow tooth--no, no
teeth or fangs or claws,
thanks. Big skies
or nothing, from here to there,
broad as China, my hands
spanning your back,
pulling you into me.

And some of that, please,
what I do when I get to do
it my way, me on top, say,
the water creeping up your body
until you drown, the sand
stretching away like the pane
of a window, like...China.
Do it or not. Cast your own curse.

Come home late,
but write the poem that denies death.
Put some aqua in it, some
damned persimmon if you have to.
Dance the syllables
down your legs and out your
few toe hairs. Dance your
knuckly body on mine,
praising whatever angel you got to
that gets you here. But
write me a poem. Make it shake,
shine like China, everyone all at once
jumping up and down in joy.

LOCUS CERULEUS

> "A blue area on the brain stem..."

If I could guess just where the March thaw
starts up, I would be a wise man with a lot of money.

As it is, I listen to the first easy grovelings
of roots from around rocks that have held

hard sway over them, hear the big relaxation
begin. Spring clatters down around us,

water loud in the spout. New birds come
every day, those away since before the world changed

color and fell apart--the smart ones, the ambitious,
those with no aptitude for monochrome, this utter lack

of flowers. For months winter has had a face--
anthracite, a cup of moonlight scattered on its brow.

A face staring from pine needles, the dead eyes
of pudding stones, the hair of a squirrel's tail,

the curled hand of an oak leaf gesturing shut.
Winter is stranger to the curve, despite

what snowdrifts say, in spite of vowels in the eaves.
The cold likes the shattered, the caws and creaks

of grackles and jays and juncos, brittle cones
of farm lights sputtering half-alive at five o'clock,

those dark mornings as we talk about what will become
of us, as we lie hard and pale against each other

beneath flannel, shadows in a cave, under the weather.
Why do we remain, year after year, cursing barrenness,

despairing of seeing another star from Nativity on,
wearing our sullen clothes, our gray brains shrinking

as small as those of mean lizards about to extinct?
Why do we put up with this crap?

Perhaps for this: Birch buds coming unglued
on the perilous first day of fifty degrees,

the return of warm ornaments hung
by claw and beak in the trees, the trees

fuzzing like antlers, raring to go, the sap moving
slowly enough so the twigs can adapt, perk up

without snapping. From inside our stucco fortress,
we look out to all this idling rouse and covert ache,

envious, hostage, and sweatered to the gills,
look out to the woods where ice ebbs enough

to free the smells of leaf rot, stagnant pool,
the autumn carcass of a rabbit caught mid-leap.

It is a dark blue place in the world's mind
awakening from a sleep as deep as the frost line,

as wide as a hemisphere, tight as a wet knot--
we are being undone by the sly hands of poplar,

falling away in an ancient, blue cognition
like a ton of bricks.

AT THE GALLERY

AVON STREET

Moving this way on Sunday is one delight:
so hot we dread touch, touch now become the daily news,
the hard-won atrocities and blare of arrogance.
This Sabbath we put ice-cubes on each other's bodies.
The cool does us proud, miming what's good and funny,
while the slick, scary magazines sprawl around us.
To love, thus, is the loneliest time.
We know we are saying good-by in a language
we know by heart yet cannot articulate.
On the simmering porch, the day an early but easy
entrance into true summer, you show me diagrams
your father showed you to prove or disprove
the charity of God, a flow chart of charisma and
    folderol.

And then this, your quick neck--is this what you prize?
Color of a lily, the taste plain as flour,
like the skin between your knuckles as you knead bread,
as you are slowly sweet to yourself,
remembering the honeysuckle by your folks' back door
back home, your mouth on those blooms, that pleasure
that is almost redemptive, almost salvation.
How violent and evocative our tools of creation:
hips, twenty-dollar typewriters from Samoa, memory.
These tubes of oils I've wasted trying to capture you--
purple, argent, ochre, and red, these attempts at
    flesh.
How wonderful, though, are we, witnesses
to the wrath and spite of it, ghosts and all.

THE PAINTER APOLOGIZES TO HIS MUSE

Finally, there was just too much canvas.
Think of it, miles of it, day in and day out,
rolling off those mills down south of here
like so much sweet grease or gentility,
a ton of bleached muslin an hour, it seemed,
pouring at me, always at me, in my face
like a month of Sunday's bad reviews,
a full calendar of friends' advice, vice.

Not to mention the tubes of paint. Picture,
if you will, every imaginable color--
enough to make you pray for insomnia just to have
time enough to pretend you knew what each is for.
God didn't need this much choice, for Christ's sake,
for sunsets, body organs, orgasms, or gasoline
spills in gutters. But, of course, this is all
subterfuge, as you know. It was the subject matter
did me in. Too much of too many good things,
and a good deal more. We desire more than we need,
and it's never enough. Wait a minute, I say to the
void
one night: Didn't the moon just do this a month ago?

The same cloak and disappearing act? Planets,
clouds, this rock on which we dance to keep
from being flung off. Such slick delight we take in,
try to capture with our fumbling hands, our
piece-meal brains and gung-ho souls. Thanks,
but no thanks. Sometimes we can't do
any more than listen: wind in the lowing pine boughs,
rain scavenging the vulnerable air, trains
filling up the hollow night. To whom do we pray--
to stop it, all of a sudden--the same carnival boys
we pray to to keep it going one more darkness?

One more paycheck, one more careless thump of the
    heart?
Let us slide through life without art
like slugs through a drain-pipe. Let us ask
the vultures how sweet it was, how sweet we were.

NARCISSUS

for James Wright

Who would have guessed: Beneath all
of last year's leaves, these pale
faces of narcissus, reflections of the louder
daffodil, mirroring the other side
of beauty. Just think, all of March they've
emerged from the earth like blonde swimmers,
face-first, white from the squeeze of water.
How blessed we are...

We wake up, put on new brown shoes,
go out testing the wind, wrapping love
around us like an indolence. We sit
in rented rooms with our appliances on,
and the hunger starts up, the horror begins.
Our brothers the child killers spread their lips
and walk down green corridors to die.
In Ohio we wait for the redbuds to crack open,
children of Judas. The mild Japonica shatters...

You knew that other side of pleasure,
the dark hemisphere of doubt and desire.
Some nights we become human only when
we absorb the drastic, learning to sanctify
ourselves above all, knowing above all,
like pale narcissus, we won't last the month.

Other nights we sit under the headlight moon
and want to have done with it. Or want
someone else to go through it painlessly
while we watch: Flowers without destination,
cracking up through the soil too early.
Too late. I walk around the homes of friends,
the caul just fallen from their eyes,
and pick up their sweet, abandoned clothes,
and breathe them in.

28

FOR DUNCAN, FOR THE WATERCOLOR, THANKS

> Whoever you are
> in the evening go outside
> out of your room
> where you know everything.
> --Rainer Maria Rilke
> from *The Book of Pictures*

So this is what
   you make of it all:
sky, trees,
   this copse of solitude,
a burnish of northern weeds.

A gift, nonetheless. And rare.
   We talk of Georgics
over empty Chinese food containers.
   We talk of failure, its wooden mask,
of what's next.

And what rage fits.
   North of here, your town
readies itself for winter;
   here: my city does the same,
as tenderly, as cruelly,
   perhaps like a remaining eye
going blind.

It is as though, D.,
   we are barbers meeting at the diner
on a Saturday evening
   comparing notes.

It is as though we are
   barbarians doing the same, encamped in front
of the cathedral, the cave,
   a kill under our belts,
the porcelain universe stretching before us,
   behind us, inside our hearts.

We each have this little forest
   just outside the window, just nearby,
like an angel we can almost touch.
   We grin at the inconstant evening stars,
pack up our booty and head for the hills.

But there's this image you leave behind:
   The drizzle of sumac wet
and overcast, the bruise and
   leit motif of autumn.

Sometimes to be an angel is all right,
   sometimes too much.
Let us look at ourselves, admiring, finally,
   what we cannot be.
But...that curve, that instant, that rush
   of thunder not too far over the horizon...
what most this warm weather lacks is a comforting wind.

EMBODIMENT

So that his earlier large canvases
should be completed entirely
out of doors, Monet required
certain trenches to be dug
so that he could reach all areas
of his earlier canvases.
Thus were certain desks created.
Thus were certain worlds made.

When I go out to sit in my car
at 3:00 a.m. I am only slightly demented.
The car is in no shape to go anywhere
and neither am I. When I sit
at my desk at any hour, life swarms
around me like locusts or Jehovah's
Witnesses or the very, very body politic
of life itself. Or swans at Ville d'Avray,

where Degas undertook a series of oil and pastel
sketches depicting laundresses at work.
I wonder about back-up lights, brake failure,
how we each die from within like stool pigeons,
pine trees, and art movements. We, you and I,
sob so separately from each other,
we must lean slightly into the night to
--if not hear--at least sense each other's
sorrow. Pretending we don't do
this too often for too many people.

Sometimes, living this close to the earth,
it's not who we want to be, but what--
hovering over the white root, the lace of plants
mattering to each other. These laundresses,
though--one of them at least: pressing the iron
down on what appears to be a shirt collar,
as though pushing her being down and into.
But the other, yawning into your face.
And her blouse about her breasts.
And that bottle of water.
And all those shadows.
And all those shadows.
And all those--no, few, colors.

AT THE BRAY GALLERY

after photographs
by Jacques-Henri Lartigue

It is Lyon, France, circa turn of the century,
and all is soon to be lost. These plump faces
of your girlfriends, high-top shoes, racing cars
at speed, their narrow, leaning oval wheels,
the bright-eyed boys with severe lips
and backward caps driving fast, all long gone.

These are what we have: so many bored people,
ready for anything, leaping for the sake
of your infernal machine, looking absent-minded
and too rich for their own good,
succumbing to your vision like an army of glamour,
new recruits mesmerized as deer
by your brass contraption, your voyeur's soul.

And in this photograph,
what will soon be a troop train chuffs in its oil
on a siding next to parasols and lean hounds.
Cramped-looking children stare at fat pigeons
pecking in the dust and cinders. There is no one
but us in the gallery. And there is only
this one last picture before we go:

A girl in color, in sunlight so hot it shakes
the day. A summer at a lake. Nothing is fugitive
but the look in her eyes. Not curve,
not the grain of light on water, nor proper
sensibility. She is about to write a letter.
She is sitting under a willow by the lake
looking over souvenirs of holidays
just before the war: Medals from school,
white silk scarves, photographs. White smoke
of trains refueling at Lyon, ornate as industry...

But what art do we see when we see each other
rapt with art? She is about to write a letter to a boy,
composing it in her radiant head, remembering
where she hid the paper, the postage, his address,
his name. But there is no artist who could capture
the thrilling, dreadful waste of a world aflame,
about to be changed forever,
scalded like a lapful of apples to deepen the hues.

WORK (AND GLOW)

SCRIPTURE

In the middle were the stiff pages,
family events listed between testaments.
They seemed more holy, as secret to me
as women's flimsys, marked with silk ribbons
no one ever used. Late at night,
I would take it under my covers
and look for my dead sister's presence
and try to imagine her now lost in the thin scripture
on either side, those pages to the left
where legends and monsters lived,
those to the right thinned with red melodrama.
I would suppose she was somewhere round and shiny
as a bullet arcing across the sheep and palm trees,
the bearded men and aching women, the calm.
Tiny leaf, brief guest of this world:
they say you were so birth-twisted it was a mercy,
face split open to the storm of this life,
brain-dead, dead. What's God like?
I can't imagine, any more than I can conjure up
the crime of your nine days of pain, the howl
already unearthly, not of our kind.
Mistake, error, carved from our mother
like a mortal blemish, hidden away, denied.
Whose bright idea were you?

CECROPIA

We are now on a walk with your father,
frail and wiry as a stripped willow branch,
as he shows us his garden and frilly orchard.
He does not yet approve of us together,
as he does not yet give much credence
to the worth of civilization or creeping
(what else?) socialism. And we are so new,
shy as mimosa to the touch, and happy.

It is spring just outside a crossroads town
in Central Ohio, the weather just warm enough
so your mother can wash the Ford in the drive,
sing about the Blood of the Lamb, air the house.
Nothing so far has achieved the first
of summer's fondness and cloy, but is growing
through the erratic intensity and blur
of breaking forth: sumac, Sweet William,
Chinese pea, and oak. Your father names
the bursting green as if they were novels.

Back by the fence on the scaly trunk
of a Golden Delicious apple tree, two Cecropia moths
mate, melding their bellies, grasping a bare branch
between their spiracles. Almost immobile,
the gates of their wings creak and stutter
on the crisp hinges of their bodies. They will not
scare. They sleep within each other, sharing
a grief, like us, out of their league,
a dumb-show of creation, figures in a poem.

TRICKS OF THE STYLISH

Autumn comes to us so resoundingly,
and yet so roundabout. Gold leaves
where none were yesterday, brass bands
in the tree-tops playing dirges.

Season of deft motion, of tactile light.
This is when item on item makes a noise,
and air has a hue--supple, a handful
of thigh. O, palpable

blue! The obituaries lengthen,
alas. Bodies we know well turn in sleep,
young boys cry out for no reason,
and we polish our windows
senselessly clean.
How else to adequately prepare?

How amazing your wise eyes, son,
when I choose to look...

On the radio we hear who'll
next be deputy of everywhere, the price
of wheat, sow bellies, faith,
anything, and how, finally,
to cope.

We learn the style and tricks
of the stylish. We argue over atoms:
What is the smallest particle
we have to worry about? And:

Do you care how I'll die? Will you keep my body near?
Will I stink or merely explode with your love
like dry kindling?

How amazing your eyes, while the world
swoons and gawks at its large hands.
Pretty eyes, my boy, vivid as one desperate
carnivore discovering a smaller one.

PRESS

This man, looking at what
is in his hands, knows just about
what to say. Give him time.

He has stood at this press
for more hours than you
or I have been awake and asleep.

While we consider how a teal
or sparrow does something special,
and does it so well, and how

in the hell we can spread our
little bit of humanity
so far--he has been talking

to his legs, saying, "Friends,
some more time, that's what I'm
asking." Look,

see?
See? How this old dog we'd
despaired of still gives us

life? Tongue pressing on us, creating
what we will be next,
or the wind pressing down on us,

imagine that! Or each of us pressing
down on each of us--imagine,
the earth in your face like a welcome wind.

It is the press my father manned
for thirty years, his steel-toed
work shoes, his uniforms of green

and khaki and teal-blue and the dance
he did for nothing, next to nothing,
for my slim applause and my urging gaze.

I'm just this small guy at my own press,
remembering someone in my off hours,
smelling the cut grass, the feel of

the heads of hunting dogs, beagles,
in my curved hand, their off-hand names
of Lady and Bugle and Melody,

the sound of how they howled for
the smallest of game. Perhaps we only lack
a syntax of praise--we have all the rest:

the need and the resolute desire to be better.
Tonight the moths man the windows,
aching for enough light to die for.

POEM BEGINNING WITH A LINE BY JANICE

> Love is a figure of speech.
> --Octavio Paz

Come inside, my mother says,
the weather is not to be
believed, needles and knives
of sleet and flurries, bird
death, rat death, all of a kind.
It's zero degrees, son, zero
prognosis, and the warm-blooded
know it, smell it like freon
spoor, the cold gray bandage
of fear scuffing round the moon.

Come inside, my mother says,
you're not quite right in the head,
son, O son, whose father is
sticking out of your every crease and
doubt, whose trash fire of a heart
grumbles shut. It's zero IQ, too,
in that empty urn of an empty head.
You should know better but you don't.
You should have known the lay of the land,
and that essence is a mindful wind.

Come inside, my mother says,
the streets run chrome and anthracite--
no safe haven for you, my careless son.
Careless with love and careless without,
the long-abandoned beacon your homing device;
just as well. There you are stuck once
again inside that poem without a clue.
Here, then, is the rain you don't understand,
here, then, too, the coat of your father,
who's just as lost, just as without name.

1945

The war as we know it is over.
   The day is as soft and gray as a fedora.
Your mother and your father are having a date.
   An outdoor cafe in New York.
They are having thick white mugs of black coffee.
   Or glasses of dark red wine.
Doughnuts.
   Cars are still scarce in the streets.
Your father isn't just back from the war.
   He didn't have to go.
He didn't have to do anything.
   Your father and your mother--but especially your
Father--
   Him in the fedora, him with his bad eyes--are
Sensitive
   About this fact.
They are not showing the right films yet at the Rialto.
   Your father's right hand rests lightly on your
Mother's
   Left.
The very first chill wind of autumn rises lightly,
   Blows by a flyer advertising a hot new jazz club.
Neither notices.
   No one does.
Your mother reaches down to straighten her stocking
   Seams.
   They are the first nylons available since the truce.
Your father notices.
   Her legs are round and long.
They lead, as he will soon come to know, toward
   Despair.
   And you.

FAMILY, EASTER PORTRAIT, 1952

1.
Looked at one way,
it's as though someone took his hand
and rubbed it across us

while the print was still wet.
We blur into one another, into
the overcast sky, into both

memory and belief. We squint
into spring sun, grouped like
reflections in a department store

window, squeezed together and tentative,
brash, but not ready for
what we're in the middle of.

2.
The gals wear corsages, the guys
their clean shirts and forced smiles
like Sunday next-to-best.

There, leaning out of the picture,
someone's dog. Here, leaning in,
a grandchild or slow cousin, birds

on a wire, fields of chicory,
a brand-new Pontiac with a wooden heart
on the rear-view mirror:

Forever is carved there. And
Always. I was seven years old.
Abstractions amazed me.

3.
Looked at another,
this is what I have to offer up, where
I come from, what I desire.

My friends and lovers
see me in all the noses and postures
and visions, the personality.

But expecially they see
the long holiday stretching
out, and the weedy grins,

and the small space that seems
to separate each and every one
in the photo, that little gray patch

that serves as edge.

CHARLIE

He expected everything. Imagine that.
On long, glowering August days
he would fathom the hard hearts
of automobiles in his garage,
insinuate his black-mooned hands
into the maze of automatic transmissions,
into the viscera of poached deer
hanging from the beams, the rain dancing
in galoshes on the corrugated steel roof above.

Half the time the customers couldn't pay,
and their cars would fill the field out back
like corpses in the rye grass and jack pine.
Half the time he would give the venison away
to Chippewa hoboes camped along the swamp.
He was my hero, skinny and bitter
in striped overalls with the knees out.

He knew things I had to know--
how to lay cement blocks for a septic tank,
twanging the plumb-line with its chalk etch
of blue, how to hammer a nail in three strokes.
How to fillet a fish and fry it
before it quite stopped wriggling.
How to drink whiskey neat in a jelly glass
all afternoon and still be able to see
a spikehorn buck along the Muskegon River
in last light and drop it to its knees
with one shot, no scope, from a hundred yards.

I didn't know any better.
I thought these were good things,
proper things for a man to know.
I was nothing like him and he knew it--
city boy who read too much,
always breaking my glasses, always
stepping on the fishing line down along
Tinny Creek where the evening brown trout
swooned under cedar logs, always complaining
about mosquitoes and blackflies and no-see-ums,
always figuring this paradise would last forever.

Some Grand Rapids executive owns it all now,
every outbuilding and rusted Chevy,
all the piss-poor land as far as you can walk
on a good day. Charlie died and was buried,
reeking still of gasoline and Canadian Club.
They said it was cancer of the balls
doing its job, working overtime,
clocking him out early,
just like an old friend would do.

WORK (AND GLOW)

He hadn't a notion
what was beyond the daily
obituaries and his job.

At the kitchen table
under a pine Camel pack
dispenser, he sat

under the clock.
A small man, but smooth,
my father affected yellow

old guy hair and work clothes.
He owned twos: two pair of shoes,
Romeos and steel-toed

brogans. Two hats,
a straw and a fedora.
Two lives: a

this one I knew, and
a that one I didn't.
In this one

he slept until noon
and was soon gone.
In that one

he lingered with women
who wore other
than housedresses.

In this one, he didn't figure.
In that one,
I guess, yeah, he did.

Who's to know?
But I can guess:
Butt of jokes,

everyone's old man, asshole?
Look:
these are his fingers

trying to twirl the micrometer,
his eyes losing depth
perception, knees shaking

in the oily pit to which
he succumbs finally. Which dad,
whose lank, dead body is lifted

to the ceiling
where dirty fluorescent lights
light up his fine Janus face?

THE MIDDLE WEST

DISPLACEMENT

My neighbor owns a big yellow boat
made of--concrete. I know, I know,
that' s not supposed to matter, of course
Anything's theoretically capable
of floating. But <u>concrete?</u>
As a matter of fact, I've never see it on a lake,
only there in the yard, the size
of a bus, beside the weeds going through
their motions, season to season, like a slow sea.
I suppose the old guy built the thing.
He's a widower, early sixties, a busy
sort of man. When it's too cold
to work outside, he can be imagined
sitting with coffee in the kitchen,
where he likes to sit, looking out
through the misted windows at his boat,
at the grim traffic nearby. Sometimes
the boat glows so bright and fierce,
it blinds him. He thinks about his wife
a lot, I know, and how they cut
the cancer away little by little
over a long summer. He remembers
the very day it hit her brain, and
she called him daddy and Audrey and
son of a bitchin bastard. What could he say?
Then the silent days began, and the harrowing
nights when he wasn't at the hospital,
when he staggered around his boat,
whiskey in a Libby glass. That was when
he started thinking about other women, too,
alone and flirting with nuttiness.

That was when he sold his guns,
even the elegant Winchester thirty-aught-six
his father gave him. All of them.
And bought, of all things, sheet music
from the forties, pornography, and food.
He began to think of women he couldn't outlive.
I'm probably wrong. I know this man as well
as my father, say, some glorious stranger
grown quirky in his dotage. Big deal,
a big yellow boat slightly awry in a field
of wild carrot and chicory, a lit
kitchen window I consider as I drive by.

ISA'S HOUSE

Rusty wringer-washer on the sloped back-porch,
fat and idle as a sultan. Sixteen cats, a harem.
Cat having kittens inside an oven.

Isa's house. Isa, as old as anyone local
cares to remember, swollen static with years,
her mind faded by half like her bleached housedress.

Improvident, we bring her casseroles and our shameful
youth. Who are we? her dark eyes ask, corneas
as violet as October evenings, calla lily cataracts,

eyes that quicken in the oil lamp flame, flicker
as she touches our faces with rough hands,
rough heart. How dare we? That night,

in the upstairs bedroom, we love as quietly
as brass on iron allows, surrounded by Depression
    glass,
yellow Colliers, a stuffed squirrel forever chewing

through the same porcelain nut, his marble eyes amazed.
We dream we are Isa's dead children, home for the
    holiday,
home to see if the memory of us still meshes

in our mother's brain. Sister and brother, we wake
into our names, our bodies twined, as sleet pings
the window, rodents frisk between walls eating
    asbestos.

TREMOR

Though the '57 Chevy my Dad
bought me was an automatic
and had four doors, much to my teen-age chagrin,
it was a hard-top with dual exhausts,
a milled cam. And mounted on that short-block
engine were two Holly four-barrel carbs.
My God, was it fast.

I heated the springs red
with a brother-in-law's stolen shop torch
until it settled just right
to cruise four inches off the ground.
I poured hot oil through
the glass-pack mufflers until,
backing down from forty in low gear,
you could hear the 283 snarling
a mile away. Or so they said.
I did this every other block.

Saturdays I would wax it all afternoon
until it glowed gold and black
and quick as a summer finch--as stark
as summer. All sweltering evening
I would wait at Walli's Drive-In
for Donald Barber to show up
in his old man's Oldsmobile.

Now I rise from your side
long past midnight some twenty-five years
later to come downstairs and write this,
as if I might ever forget it.
The dark air outside over the fields
is solid and nearly starless.

In the black and flaring distance
I hear the C & O and Grand Trunk
Western trains torqueing slowly through
unmarked crossings. And hot yellow
cars winding up tight to red line
on the back roads out of here.
All of us, every one of us, looking for
a state of grace or the state line,
whichever comes first before morning.

ROSALIE

1.
She just stands there, feet
black from leaked oil, sawdust
specks on her red chipped
toe nail polish, the old red
pegasus rampant on the cement
block wall, and she sucks
her bad gums, looking out
to the gas vapors swirling
around him, his big dumb ears,
his big dumb cock loose
in his overalls, he's so dumb
and worthless, his hair
combed back, sinister -like,
in waves of brilliantine, and
she breathes it in, the ethanol
and her hot breath and the evening
sprung around her like a universe
going wacky with all these
new stars, and this twenty dollar
bill she got from the UPS trucker
for doing next to nothing, saying
nothing, saying O.

2.
Carbondale sky,
brimming with the buzz and
waddle of late August, her
in her thin print dress,
alone in a puckerbush field,
hot as living hell, crows
on the updraft, fat and silly
in the heat, she says her name
and the last name of her beau,
and a wind blows in from
the clay mines empty since May,
and she would be happy enough
for this to be it forever,
face flushed with desire,
hands in her pockets
feeling her round thighs,
her mons, its crisp hair,
her lips, then her belly where
the child kicks once, and
for the last time. What
did we know, there we all were,
looking on.

3.
Yellow air, sluggish clouds,
and far-off cries of mothers
calling kids home from
baseball and kick-the-can.
Otherwise, a silence,
as though it all were inside
a world, a whole bouquet
of birds flying up
and out like a gratitude.
Inside a world, mind you,
that soon will allow
pin-pricks of another through.
Onto
this one, ragged with
cocker spaniels, whiffs
of brush fires, blond
cowlicks, and the dust from
an iron bed where a man
throws his wife down on it,
and, say, shoots her,
again and again, and then
the neighbor's child,
Rosalie, and then himself.

THE MAN WITHOUT A NOSE

Sometimes he wears a shiny prosthesis--
poreless and pink. Often he wears a bandage,
his profile like a time-abused Etruscan bust,
unearthed, ensconced on a pedestal.

Once in a while he wears nothing,
facing a cringing world that quibbles
each morning over size and modulation,
that worries over insidious hairs
and blotches, the broken capillaries
of drink, yearning for the Aquiline flare.
His vengeance is just.

Once there was the shirred bitterness
of marigolds rampant around his mother's
cedar-shake house, her bending in pain
in a furious chemise, to pluck the dead
yellow heads for next spring's planting.
Later, her legs tucked up, defined
by muslin sheets, he smelled the welfare
clinic's smells--turquoise plastic,
benzocaine, and jello with radish bits.
The smell of her dentures when they kissed.

No perfect nose, no band-aid, he loves
to watch the clerk in the convenience store
squirm in her short stretch skirt
as he orders his filterless Kools
and remembers the musky lotion another woman
used to spread on her long body before bed.
He would pretend sleep, she would pretend
he slept, and slide her hands up his thighs
and hold him against the bad business
of the night ahead.

And the reek of her mouth afterwards,
smell of the sea, ammonia of the beginning
of life on her tongue... In his room
at the Berridge Hotel, he holds his hands
before his carved face like ripe carrion,
fragrant lovers and mother for his flesh,
only, for his dreams of flesh.

THE DRAGGERS

We try to sit and breathe
between our turns
at the rope and hooks

We feel the sweet rubbed wood
of the boat seat on our butts,
smell the water,

watch the greening trees
on shore propose summer. To
look forward to pulling

out of the river something
swollen twice its size, and gray:
We have our calling,

and we have our price.
Once I lived
for the shimmer of a nylon line

drawn taut between me
and a trout, the Crayola red
and yellow bobber disappearing...

I wake in dreams of seaweed
sliding endlessly
from the mouths of your loved ones.

DAGUERRE

This photograph,
palsy caught,
jaundice amplified
into resolute sunlight,
its late slant
up the wall.

All sinew,
synapse, attenuation
of spirit
once more proved
ineluctable.

The eyes go wild,
illumined from within
like cathedrals,
the insane,
saints.

Ill-cut clothes,
scuffed brogans, typhoid
and pox preventatives
emanating from every
pore, buttonhole, crease...

We know exactly
what they'd be like
were they alive now,
scratching and fidgeting,
bad breath,
their coal mine cough,
factory grime, rusty
fork on brown teeth,
and the sucked pipe.

But holy,
the women dressed in drab
to cover bruises,
the scald of dreariness,
the men drained of all
force save ignorance.
But holy,
the children mild
and ephemeral, so close
to death they blur.

DIME

1.
The evening calls begin with
a man lost in a city he knows
like a bad dream--though who
would have guessed, strung out so
his hands may as well be kids
he left in St. Louis, how many
wives ago, how many women,
all those bottles, if he only
had a dime for each. Some gals
those gals, Mona, and what's
her name, and Camomile (he swears),
her and her ruddy thighs and cough,
Jesus, now look at him, sixty
years of this shit and no job,
nothing, can't even get it up,
can't even get up north where
Mona lives, he's heard, don't you
have another goddamn number
I can call, somebody who'll
do something, make it right, make it
all worth my while, tell somebody,
I'm down to it now, buddy.

2.
Oh, and she was something,
the next one says, slim and
fragile as those porcelain
doodads her mother had
on the dressing table, eyes
as clear as church windows,
even though you'd never guess it
now, what with these sores,
this gimpy leg, but I was a prize,
I was his baby girl and he said
he'd hurt me for it if I told
mama before he up and left us,
and life is something you treasure,
ain't it, even when it ain't worth
a dime and you ain't got a pot
to piss in, and oh sure
I think about ending it sometimes,
maybe plenty, but you got to hang
tough, make it to your next check,
you never know when a man
might need you.

3.

And just before the shift change
the last one is crying and
I can't understand a word, so
I listen and it's a comfort,
I suspect, just to have me on
the line, just to have a connection,
and, hey, I'm in no hurry, no place
special to go, and what the hell,
it's their dime, so I just make
my presence known, making little
sweet sounds so as to show I'm
still here, and I croon some song
I like whose words I forget,
and I'm almost at a good place, too--
all those smells and flavors,
warmth and flesh and safety,
and you know how you can remember
what might not have been so hot
all that long time ago, except now,
who knows, it's exactly what you need,
you couldn't ask for anything
better, and it's all for free,
free for the asking.

CHEESE LINES, FLINT, MICHIGAN

Gray lines of women at the North Flint Plaza--
waiting their due, surplus cheese and butter
we can't use, the lines that shuffle
down the weed-split sidewalks,
past the boarded-up display windows
of The Fair, United Shirt, Nobil Shoes,
while at the curb monstrous green Buicks
idle and rust. The day is overcast,
threatening drizzle, feinting autumn
and further calamity. I drive by, this,
my old neighborhood, this shopping center,
our hang-out--vanilla root beers
at the drug store, a pack of Luckies secreted
behind a loose brick, our leather jackets
with The Royals on the back,
our pointed Flagg Bros. shoes, and D.A. hair.
We the pioneers. These the women we went
to school with who never moved away,
who we never spoke to, let alone desired.
Or desired, but never let on.
                                        Flint, a city
as hard and abrupt as its quick bitten name.
Home of Chevy in the Hole, where men
like my father got used to days
etched thin and gritty as Mohawk vodka
and steel shavings in their thick aching hands
and little wretched patches of back yards
where they maybe played catch with
their kids before second-shift.
See how easily those women are forgotten,
even in poems devoted to their bad luck.

GETTING MY FATHER OUT

The two boys out in the ambulance
are passing a joint. I can see them
through the trailer window.

They are nodding their heads
to some Twisted Sister song on the radio,
smiling, sitting out there
in the late June sun,

and I am in here to get my father out.
He is dead, so there isn't much
need to hurry, yet I wish they would.

He is in the back bedroom
beside the bed, I am out here,
they are out there. This is a still-life,
I tell myself. I look around:

an ashtray of thumbed-out Camels,
a TV Guide with Ed Asner on the cover,
my father's Romeo house-slippers
under his chair. The day is a dazzler
and I would rather be elsewhere,

on a lake, back in bed, anywhere.
But the park super called me and said,
Something's wrong, and she was right.

And now I have to tell everyone.
I'll hate that. Maybe not as much
as walking into his bedroom
and finding him on the floor staring at
infinity with his mouth open in surprise
or fear--but almost.

I mean, I got out of there, and right away--
it took two seconds, tops.
But calling all those people and telling them...
Aunt Agatha with her rouge and black shoes,
Uncle Florence with his...tubes. The rest.

That's what's so bad about death.
Not the body--hey, I can live with that--
but the phonecalls and the arrangements
and never knowing what folks will say.

I think the boys are coming now.
They're not smiling, though I can tell
they're stoned. That must be difficult, too.
They'll understand what I'm going through.

You know, I've always liked the idea of
AMBULANCE spelled backwards on the front of it:
Language meant for mirrors instead of real life.

THE MIDDLE WEST

1.
How strange that sounds!

What is it, anyway?
The clank of plow tine on dirt, hard as iron?
The clank of stars on Rapid City,
when you step outside, all not right
with the world, middle of the night,
middle of March?

Teenage boys coveting sheep in Iowa,
sons of fundamentalist ministers
picking Better Boy tomatoes for their mamas,
out to make the whole universe Iowa.

Teen-age boys in Chicago
stealing cars, pumping iron, shooting meth,
shooting off the backs of their heads
behind billboards advertising the Rotary
and the NRA.

The Middle West.
What an idea!
All is either leaden or bright, the in-between
lost in translation,
whatever Machiavelli never bothered with.
This is the land of the spurious,
of slush and sparrows,
expressways and secreted brown pint bottles.

Nowhere land where everybody lives.

Where we drink like Russians
and look like Russians
and hate Russians more than poetry or New York.

Well, at least the Middle West
knows how to have sex:
lots of it and regular, fast and sweaty.

2.
In another room of this house,
as though across the county line,
is a table, highly polished,
gleaming like a casket. On it,
a linen cloth figured with small
fleur-de-lis. On it,
gilt picture frames. In them,
Marines, graduates, babies,
and dead pets, eyes afire
in the camera flash, tongues out
in the July heat.

You want to ask,
Who are these folks of the Middle West?
And: Why do you hear reggae music
from this window in Kalamazoo?
Why is this blind woman starving
in a shit-filled basement in Springfield?
Why is Ohio so big?
Why don't we have any lips to speak of?
In the dark rooms of the Tittabawasee River,
why aren't the poets dancing?

3.
What metaphor to believe?

O, this Middle West that I love
is a large implement sale
on a bankrupt farm just off
the freeway near to closing for the day.
The last customers line up
to buy knick-knacks and baling twine,
tired and quarrelsome,
looking a bit divorced around the eyes.

O, this Middle West that I love
is like a dog in a movie--
acting as though it were in real life,
while everyone else is pretending.

4.
We knew, sure as hell, not five miles
out from town, newly-hatched starlings
were opening their eyes in ditches
and wondering at the Fruehauf trucks
busting past, the reflective off-ramp
signs shining the way to Valhalla,
pointing the way to the stockcar speedway--
O Middle West heaven on earth!

Let us sit at the southwest corner
of the track, where if there's going to be
a howdy-do with death we'll feel it,
surrounded by women in Pennzoil jackets,
men reliving the Korean War,
their self-inflicted tattoos,
blear-eyed children ready to replace them
when they bludgeon each other
into this fallow ground.

O, amorous and golden Middle West!

It is a sadness not to be borne
by the likes of us.
Well, yes, to be borne.
Like a sickle through the heart.

A BLESSING FOR POETS:
GOING JOHN KEATS ONE BETTER

> "If poetry comes not as naturally as the leaves
> to a tree, it had better not come at all."

May the poems come as easily
as these many brown birds
to the branch still bare as though
it thought winter was still
the way of the world, as easily
as a fall of water down through
tropical air to the palm of a stone
waiting with its one cupped thought
eroding larger, as easily as the thoughts
of lilacs to the air, iris
to the air, wild roses to the air,
like one big idea of sweetness.

May the words you desire
fall upon you like unexplained sadness,
thankfulness, and grace, as easily
as lips on the nape of a neck
where the hair smells of balsam
and morning, mimosa and pine,
as easily as the wind through pine needles
like a song through teeth,
through cedar boughs, down and down
to the valley where no one can sleep
for laughing and kissing,
except the dead who are also pleased.

As easily as dreams
of your mother, still alive,
still in her rocker on the porch,
worried you won't come home
in one piece, worried you will
break your neck, marry wrong,
run out of money, be like your dad.

May the poems come as easily as any two things
meant to be one come together.

Danny Rendleman teaches writing at the University of Michigan-Flint. *The Middle West* is his sixth book of poetry. He is the recipient of three Arts Foundation of Michigan/Michigan Council for the Arts grants. He lives in Flint with his wife, Jan Worth.